CESAR CHAVEZ

DAVID R. COLLINS

**In Consultation with Martha Cosgrove,
M.A. and Reading Specialist**

JUST THE FACTS BIOGRAPHIES

LERNER PUBLICATIONS COMPANY/MINNEAPOLIS

Martha Cosgrove has a master's degree from the University of Minnesota in secondary education, with an emphasis on developmental and remedial reading. She is licensed in 7–12 English and language arts, developmental reading, and remedial reading. She has had several works published, and she gives numerous state and national presentations in her areas of expertise.

Lerner Publications Company
A division of Lerner Publishing Group
241 First Avenue North
Minneapolis, Minnesota U.S.A.

Website address: www.lernerbooks.com

Library of Congress Cataloging-in-Publication Data

Collins, David R.
    Cesar Chavez / by David R Collins.
      p.   cm. – (Just the facts biographies)
    Includes bibliographical references and index.
    ISBN: 0-8225-2248-9 (lib. bdg. : alk. paper)
    1. Chavez, Cesar, 1927–Juvenile literature. 2. Labor leaders–United States–Biography–Juvenile literature. 3. Migrant agricultural laborers–Labor unions–United States–Officials and employees–Biography–Juvenile literature. 4. Mexican American History–Juvenile literature. 5. United Farm Workers History–Juvenile literature. I. Title. II. Series.
    HD6509.C48C648 2005
    331.88'13'092–dc22   2004023202

Manufactured in the United States of America
1 2 3 4 5 6 – JR – 10 09 08 07 06 05

Contents

IN THE FIELDS

**(Above)
Farmworkers
harvest
carrots in
the 1930s.**

SLOWLY, ELEVEN-YEAR-OLD Cesar Chavez
stood on his toes. He stretched his body in the bright
sunlight. His muscles ached. He wiped his sweat-
covered face with the thin sleeve of his shirt. He had
been picking peas in the field for three hours. But the
heat made it seem more like ten hours. The minutes
dragged along slowly, almost as slowly as the peas
piled up in the bottom of Cesar's basket.

The boy looked over at his father and mother.
They were both bent at the waist, picking peas and

putting them in their own baskets. Nearby, his brothers and sisters did the same. Once the baskets were full, other workers sorted the peas, throwing away those that could not be sold. The pea pickers got credit only for the good peas. In three hours of work, the entire Chavez family earned very little money.

Young Cesar Chavez didn't think about money while he picked peas with the other workers. Instead, he liked to remember the times before his family had to move from place to place harvesting crops.

EARLY YEARS

Cesar Estrada Chavez was born March 31, 1927, above his family's grocery store near Yuma, Arizona. He was the oldest boy in the family. Cesar was named after his grandfather, Cesario, who had fled poverty in Mexico

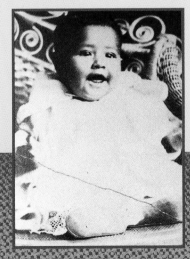

Cesar was only nine months old when this photograph was taken.

in the 1880s. Both of young Cesar's parents had been born in Mexico. They spoke mostly Spanish at home. They belonged to the Roman Catholic faith.

IT'S A FACT!

Cesar's parents, Librado and Juana, came from big families. As a boy growing up near Yuma, Cesar was surrounded by more than one hundred cousins, aunts, and uncles.

Cesar's father, Librado Chavez, was a busy man. He ran a pool hall, where people played pool. In addition to his grocery store, he owned a gas station. He also helped on his parents' farm. Cesar's father often worked sixteen hours a day. But he was never too tired to make toys for his children.

Juana Chavez, Cesar's mother, kept close watch over the family too. A small woman with long black hair, Juana was known for her big heart. To Juana, being a good Roman Catholic meant more than just going to Mass (church

IT'S A FACT!

Cesar and Richard often played in their father's pool hall. Both became skilled pool players.

Cesar and his older sister Rita

services) every week. It meant helping people every day. For example, sometimes she sent out Cesar and his younger brother, Richard, to look for people who didn't have enough to eat. She shared the family's food with them.

Cesar's mother was a gifted storyteller, even though she couldn't read or write. She shared her proverbs (short stories that carry a piece of advice) with her children. Each proverb demanded careful thought. Juana warned her children to pay attention to her advice. Of all his mother's proverbs, Cesar best remembered her advice about getting along with others. She didn't agree with fighting.

A Changing World

In the 1930s, people in the United States were living through the hardships of the Great Depression. Businesses and banks were failing across the nation. Many people had lost their jobs.

At the same time, a bad drought, or dry spell, had hit the southwestern United States, where Yuma was located. The Gila River, once full and flowing, dried up. Fields could no longer support crops. The corn and squash crops on the Chavez family farm died. Few customers came into the pool hall and the grocery store. No one in the area had money to spend. Without crops and customers, the Chavez family struggled to pay its bills.

The Gila River flowed near the Chavez farm.

In 1932, Librado, Juana, and their children moved back to Librado's childhood farm home. Although Cesar's grandfather was no longer living, his grandmother, called Mama Tella, still lived in the house. Mama Tella was very religious. At night, the Chavez children would gather around her to pray. She taught them about the Catholic faith. She

told them stories about Catholic saints and the
Virgin of Guadalupe.

On the farm, Cesar had chores. The farmhouse
didn't have indoor plumbing, so Cesar brought in
pails of fresh water every morning. He fed the
family's animals, mainly horses, cows, and chickens.
He gathered eggs from the hens.

THE VIRGIN OF GUADALUPE

The Virgin of Guadalupe
represents Mary, the mother of
Jesus. Throughout Mexico, she is
honored as the supporter of
native Indian peoples after the
Spanish Empire took over Mexico
in the early 1500s. The story is
told that in 1531 Mary appeared
to Juan Diego, a poor Indian
man. He described her as looking
like a young Indian woman. She
told Juan about her desire to
love and protect the peoples of
Mexico. For hundreds of years,
the Virgin of Guadalupe has been
a unifying force for Hispanic
Roman Catholics.

Even though the Chavez family had food,
money was still scarce. Many families bartered
(traded one thing for another) instead of paying
cash, and the Chavezes were no exception.
Librado continued to struggle to scrape together
the money to pay the taxes on his businesses and
the farm.

For a while, the state government allowed
him to put off paying the taxes. But in 1937, the
struggle ended. The State of Arizona demanded
that Librado pay what he owed. When Librado
couldn't pay, he was ordered out of his home
and off his land. The farm that his family had
run for many years was sold to a large
landowner. The Chavez family had to take up a
different way of life.

BECOMING A MIGRANT FAMILY

In 1938, Librado headed to California, joining
thousands of other Americans who had also lost
their farms. Many of these ex-farmers became
migrant farmworkers. Many of the migrants were
Americans of Hispanic heritage. They moved
from town to town in search of work. For low
pay, the migrant workers harvested crops for farm

Children play in front of housing for migrant workers in California in 1940.

owners. As soon as he could, Librado sent for his wife and children.

As migrant workers, the Chavez family lived in small, run-down shacks or in tents in crowded camps. Often they had no plumbing or electricity. The children had nowhere to play. Cesar and his brothers and sisters attended school for a few weeks at a time, until a crop was harvested. Then the family moved on. Cesar constantly fought to keep up with his lessons.

At home, everyone spoke Spanish. But in school, all students had to speak English. In fact, teachers punished students who spoke Spanish in school. The teachers didn't respect or appreciate the Mexican heritage that many of the students

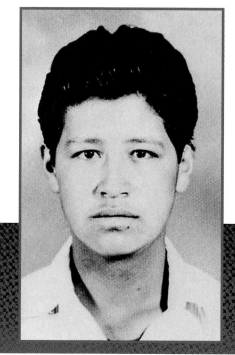

Cesar as a young man

had. As a result, Cesar didn't enjoy school. He was always glad when the school day was over.

Some of Cesar's friends fished in California's rivers for fun. But Cesar fished to help feed his family. He picked wild mustard greens too, regularly carrying home full baskets. He and Richard collected tinfoil from empty cigarette packages to earn spending money. They rolled the foil into a giant ball. The ball weighed eighteen pounds when they took it to a junk dealer. They used the money they received to buy a pair of tennis shoes and two sweatshirts.

Librado and Juana appreciated their sons' help. Earning a living back in Yuma had never been easy. But a migrant farmworker's life was much more difficult. Every penny helped the family survive. Every day meant a new search for work.

Whenever Librado heard about another crop to be harvested, he packed up his family. They drove their car to the farm that needed workers. Sometimes they arrived too late. All the workers were hired. Sometimes so many migrants needed jobs that the grower reduced the pay offered to each worker. More than once, the entire Chavez family worked for a whole day and earned only a dollar or two.

From the beginning, Cesar hated being a migrant worker. After all, he had known a different way of life. Back in Arizona, he knew his family was always struggling to pay bills. But at least they were free to live their own lives. To Cesar, migrants were chained to their way of life. The only thing that changed was the crop to be harvested.

Juana Chavez kept up the family's spirits. No one was allowed to complain. She reminded her family that others were worse off than the Chavezes. At times, that was hard

Juana Chavez greatly influenced her son Cesar.

for Cesar to believe. Cesar wore his shoes until they fell apart. Then he walked barefoot, squishing his feet in the mud. He sometimes slept under bridges when the migrant worker villages were full.

LIFE IN SAN JOSE

Eventually, the family found a more permanent home. Many fields and orchards were located around San Jose, California, south of San Francisco. The area's landowners often hired migrant workers. Librado found a small house in a Spanish-speaking neighborhood, or barrio, and moved his family there. The area was called Sal Si Puedes, which meant "get out if you can" in Spanish. Cesar soon discovered what the saying meant. Few people ever earned enough money to get out of Sal Si Puedes. The neighborhood was crowded. People had no privacy, no time to be alone.

Many of the migrant workers were growing tired of the poor living conditions, the long hours,

IT'S A FACT!

Later in his life, Cesar would use *Sí se puede* as a motto. This Spanish phrase means, "Yes, it can be done."

and the low pay. Librado and other farmworkers joined labor unions. The unions were made up of groups of people doing the same job. A union of field-workers could bargain with farm owners as a group, not one by one. Union members hoped that growers might pay more attention to demands that came from a large group of workers.

Sometimes union members came to the Chavez house to meet. Cesar listened to people talk about their jobs and lives. Discussions became shouting matches, as tired workers shared their anger and frustration. Finally, Librado and other union members demanded changes from the growers. When the growers wouldn't listen, union members went on strike.

But during a strike, workers refuse to work, so they don't get paid. Stikers hope that by striking they will force the growers to give in to their demands. At the same time, though, without farmworkers the crops don't get harvested on time, and they rot. The growers can't sell the spoiled crops and lose money. Both sides take risks during a strike.

The strikers hoped the growers would meet the union's demands. But the growers stood firm. They would not give in to the workers' demands. Day and night, the workers marched, carrying posters and shouting their demands. Eventually, their money and patience ran out. They gave up their strike and went back to work. No changes resulted from the strike.

Young Cesar wondered if workers could ever win a strike. He'd seen them spend all that time marching and shouting for change. Yet everyone went back to work with nothing to show for it. Cesar knew the workers wanted more respect and more money. By striking, the workers lost wages. They sent their children to bed hungry. An empty stomach and watching your hungry children, Cesar realized, made it hard to fight.

CHAPTER 2
TROUBLED TIMES

IN 1942, TRAGEDY STRUCK the
Chavez family. Librado was hurt in a car
accident. During his long recovery, he was
unable to work. Cesar, as the oldest son, made
a big decision. The fifteen-year-old boy left
school. He had only been able to finish eighth
grade. Once things were better at home, Cesar
planned to complete his education. His mother
wasn't happy with the decision, but she

(Above) Cesar
was able to
graduate from
eighth grade.
He never went
to high school.

understood why he had made it. With Librado out of work, the family needed money.

GROWING UP

In the fields and at home, Cesar took on more responsibility. In the past, Librado had decided when and where the family would move to harvest a crop. But Cesar began making these decisions. He seemed to have a good understanding of when to move and which growers would pay the best wages. The calendar for the Chavez family revolved around crops, and Cesar knew which crops were harvested in which times of the year.

Cesar (right) poses with his brother Richard (left) and a friend.

At sixteen, Cesar took over driving the family car, a 1930 Studebaker. Richard handled the mechanical end, setting the spark plugs and keeping the engine oiled. Cesar became part of a Mexican American group called the pachucos. Pachucos wore the colorful, oversized zoot suit, which had become popular in the 1940s. They spoke their own slang and typically thought their parents were old-fashioned.

THE ZOOT-SUIT RIOTS

In 1942 and 1943, the death of a pachuco caused a backlash against zoot-suited Mexican American youths in the Los Angeles area. The media made the Hispanic teenagers sound violent. When some U.S. sailors stationed near Los Angeles said pachucos had attacked them, other sailors responded by seeking out anyone wearing a zoot suit. Members of the Los Angeles police and the sailors arrested hundreds of Mexican Americans, not only pachucos but anyone they thought might be dangerous.

This teenage boy shows off his zoot suit in 1943.

Sometimes their rebellious ways turned violent, but Cesar chose to stay away from violence.

Even after Librado recovered some of his strength and returned to the fields, Cesar kept his new duties. He continued to follow the yearly round of melon picking, broccoli harvesting, cherry picking, and beet topping. Finally in 1944, the seventeen-year-old boy could take no more. While thinning out a row of sugar beets one day, Cesar suddenly told his father that he'd had enough of crop harvesting.

Cesar marched off the farm and didn't stop marching until he'd reached the local recruiting office of the U.S. Navy. At that time, the United States was involved in World War II (1939–1945). Cesar hoped that the navy would offer him new opportunities.

He soon learned that most Hispanic sailors served as deckhands. These workers did many of the cleaning tasks aboard a ship. While World War II raged, Cesar went from boat to boat. Sometimes he worked at sea. Other times his ship docked in a harbor. He was seasick much of the time.

COMING HOME

Cesar welcomed any break from his service and was glad to return home on shore leave. During

Cesar joined the U.S. Navy at age seventeen.

one visit to Delano, California, where his family was living, Cesar and some friends went to a movie. All the movie theaters around Delano were segregated. This meant that white people sat in the best seats nearest the movie screen while everyone else sat farther away. No laws said this, but it was understood. On this night, Cesar didn't want to sit in a segregated section. He was in uniform, and he just wanted to have a good time. Despite an usher's warning, he sat down in a seat that was off-limits to nonwhites.

Minutes later, the manager of the movie house asked Cesar to move. He refused to budge. Finally, the manager called the police. The officers pulled Cesar from his seat and took him to jail.

For the next hour, Cesar waited while the desk sergeant at the police station tried to figure out how

Cesar (far left) made friends in the navy. But he didn't serve in a battle.

to charge the young sailor. Cesar wasn't drunk. He wasn't disturbing others. He hadn't broken any written law.

When Cesar was finally set free, he was angry because of what had happened. He was also angry with himself for not doing more to fight against the unfair treatment. But for the first time, he'd stood up for his rights. Somehow, he knew more incidents like this one would happen in the future. He promised himself that, next time, he would know what to do.

IT'S A FACT!

Cesar never fought in a battle while in the navy. The closest he came was when he was in the Pacific Ocean's Mariana Islands, but the fighting was still far away.

CHAPTER 3

SEEKING DIRECTION

**(Above)
Juana and
Librado
Chavez lived
in Delano,
California, in
the 1940s.**

IN 1945, WORLD WAR II ENDED. Soon, Cesar's time in the navy was over. Nineteen-year-old Cesar rejoined his parents, sisters, and brothers in Delano. He was happy to be back home with his family and with his mother's good cooking. He smiled and laughed and was the same Cesar his family had known. The only real difference was he'd grown a mustache.

CESAR AND HELEN

Soon after his return, Cesar began spending time with Helen Fabela. The two had dated for several years, and Cesar enjoyed being with the dark-haired beauty. Like Cesar, Helen came from a big family. Although her parents weren't migrant workers, they did work in the fields, cutting cotton for a Delano farmer. Because Cesar didn't have much money, the two went on cheap dates. They took moonlight walks or went to the movies. They enjoyed being together, no matter what they did.

IT'S A FACT!

Juana welcomed Cesar home from the war by making spicy hot burritos. Cesar's favorite food. Cesar couldn't get enough.

Once again, Cesar lived his life by the harvest calendar. In the summer, he headed to the vineyards to pick grapes. During the winter, he picked cotton. When he could, he saved a little money for a special occasion.

That occasion came in 1948 when Cesar asked Helen to marry him. She agreed. They got married in Reno, Nevada, on October 22, 1948, in front of

IT'S A FACT!

On their honeymoon, Cesar and Helen toured the California missions. Spanish priests had founded the missions in the 1700s as a way to bring native peoples into the Roman Catholic Church.

a justice of the peace. Then the couple returned to San Jose, California, for a church wedding. After a two-week honeymoon trip, Cesar and Helen settled into a new life.

For the next few years, Cesar took whatever work he could find. He harvested grapes in the vineyards outside Delano and picked apricots near San Jose. The work was always hard, and the pay was disappointing.

All the same, Cesar and Helen found much to celebrate, including the birth of a son, Fernando, and then a daughter, Sylvia. The couple enjoyed their children, but Cesar quickly discovered that money was a bigger problem with children in the house. And soon, Helen was pregnant again.

CRESCENT CITY

Tired of migrant work, Cesar walked the streets of San Jose. He visited any store or business that

Cesar and Helen in 1948, shortly after they were married

might need a worker. The jobs were filled. Then he heard that a lumber factory in Crescent City, California, needed help. Cesar didn't know exactly where Crescent City was, but he was going to find out. He thought that anything would be better than working in the fields.

Cesar, Richard, and three of their cousins jumped in a car and drove north. Crescent City was four hundred miles away, along the coast.

All of them were willing to take a chance on being hired.

The chance paid off. The factory hired them. Except for when he was in the navy, Cesar was earning money away from the fields for the first time in his life. The lumber work was harder than any planting and picking Cesar had ever done. At the

Lumber workers prepare redwood logs to be taken to a sawmill in northern California.

end of each day, all he could do was fall onto a cot and sleep until the next morning.

But as Cesar and Richard got used to the work, their jobs became easier. The weekly paychecks were also welcome.

IT'S A FACT!

Forests of redwood trees—the tallest plants in the world— were also part of the environment of Crescent City.

Richard, always the handyman, started building a small house so they could bring their families from San Jose. Soon after Helen arrived in Crescent City, she gave birth to a daughter, Linda.

With a steady paycheck coming in and with his wife and three young children surrounding him, Cesar felt satisfied with his life. He just wished that it didn't rain so much in far northwestern California. Almost every day brought a downpour, and the coastal winds howled all winter. For a year and a half, Cesar and his family put up with the bad weather.

RETURN TO SAN JOSE

In 1952, Cesar learned that job openings existed for lumber workers in San Jose. He didn't need to be convinced to go back home. Cesar and Richard both gathered their families and headed south. Once back in Sal Si Puedes, Richard decided to work on his own as a carpenter. Cesar was hired at a lumber mill.

At about this time, Cesar met Father Donald McDonnell. The Roman Catholic priest said Mass for the migrant workers around San Jose. Cesar helped Father McDonnell fix up an old hall where he could hold Mass. Side by side, the two men hammered and painted old benches. As they worked, they talked and shared ideas. Both men were about the same age, and both knew a lot about migrants. Cesar had spent years working in the fields, while the priest had studied and learned through books and articles. The priest shared all he had read and learned. Cesar learned a great deal from him.

Father McDonnell was always willing to loan books to Cesar. The reading was not always easy, but the priest was there to answer questions. Cesar became interested in the economy of farming. He quickly found out that farming was much more than planting and harvesting. Farmers had to understand rules about bank loans so they could buy land, equipment, and seeds.

Cesar read about more than just agriculture. He also read about people who had helped to fight injustice. He enjoyed reading about the

gentle and humble Saint Francis of Assisi. About eight hundred years ago, Francis, an Italian Catholic, had devoted his life to feeding and helping the poor. Cesar also read about Mohandas Gandhi, a lawyer from India. More than eighty years ago, Gandhi

Cesar Chavez was inspired by the work of Mohandas Gandhi.

IT'S A FACT!

Cesar realized that Francis of Assisi and Mohandas Gandhi were much like his own mother. They were always reaching out to help the poor and always trying to keep the peace among people.

had used nonviolent action—such as going on hunger strikes—to win more rights for India's people. Eventually, his actions led to independence from Great Britain for the Indian people.

Cesar admired men and women who helped others. He wanted to help people too. People who knew Cesar often sensed that he was there to help. When people spoke to him, he listened to every word they said. He passed along what he had read and what Father McDonnell had told him. Wherever Cesar went, he attracted a crowd.

THE CSO

In June of 1952, a man named Fred Ross came to Sal Si Puedes looking for Cesar. Ross was an organizer for the Community Service Organization (CSO). Ross's job was to help people living in California's Mexican American barrios. He met Father McDonnell, who told him about Cesar. Ross asked other locals about people who might be able to help him. They also told him to talk to Cesar Chavez.

But Cesar didn't want to talk to Ross. Others like Ross had come to the barrio, claiming they wanted to help Mexican American families. The visitors always asked lots of questions and then disappeared. Their visits never helped anyone. Cesar didn't believe Ross's visit would be any different.

Cesar hid from Ross. He went across the street to Richard's house whenever the community organizer knocked on his door. But Ross kept coming back. Finally, Helen grew tired of the hide-and-seek game. She pointed out Richard's house, and Ross finally found Cesar.

Once the two men sat down to talk, Cesar changed his mind. Ross did seem different from others who had come. He seemed honest. Cesar

IT'S A FACT!

Fred Ross set up the first CSO office in Los Angeles as a self-help group for the Mexican American community. One of the main goals of the CSO was to train members to be able to help themselves and then to train others.

Cesar and Fred Ross *(left)* **became lifetime friends.**

thought that he really did want to help Mexican Americans. By the time their meeting had ended, Cesar had offered his home as a place for Ross to talk with families from the barrio. But Cesar still wasn't sure he trusted Ross. Later, he talked to a few of his friends and made a plan. If Ross said anything out of line, Cesar would make a move with his hand. That move was a signal to tell Ross to leave.

Cesar never gave that signal. From the moment Fred Ross started speaking at the meeting, he showed his understanding of barrio residents and their lives. He talked about a big meat-packaging company. It was dumping waste into a creek behind Sal Si Puedes. Many children played in the creek and developed sores. Huge swarms of mosquitoes lived in the area. Ross said the government could kill the insects but hadn't done so. The CSO was trying to fix these problems. He talked about other CSO programs and suggested how Mexican Americans could help themselves.

Cesar walked Ross out to his car after the meeting. Cesar had many questions. How could he go about organizing people in his neighborhood to gain power? What should he do next? Ross invited Cesar to another CSO meeting, and they left together.

Cesar was eager to hear more of Ross's ideas. He wanted to study the way Ross presented them. Ross strongly believed that even poor people could have power over their lives.

That night, June 9, 1952, was a turning point in Cesar Chavez's life. He wanted to organize

Mexican Americans, just as Fred Ross was doing. But it would not be easy. Cesar didn't have Ross's education and experience. But he had something that Ross didn't have. He knew the people. He was one of them. He understood their thinking, their hopes, and their dreams. Surely that counted for something. Maybe the rest could be learned. Just the thought of helping his people earn more money and get better working conditions gave Cesar new hope for the future.

CHAPTER 4

ANOTHER KIND OF HARVEST

CESAR LOOKED DOWN at the papers on the table in front of him. Some sheets were lists of names. Others were maps and graphs. Fred Ross explained what was on each sheet of paper. Cesar listened as he explained each fact, each statistic, and each law about voting. Cesar began to understand that many

(Above) Cesar learned a lot from Fred Ross in the 1950s and 1960s.

39

Mexican Americans were not voting. Cesar and Ross believed that people didn't realize how important their votes were.

GETTING PEOPLE TO VOTE

Voting represented power. Only registered voters got to decide who would run the government and make laws. If Mexican Americans wanted their needs to be heard, they needed to vote.

With that thought in mind, Cesar walked door-to-door in San Jose. He talked to Mexican Americans who were not registered (signed up) to vote. No matter how tired he was after working at the lumberyard during the day, Cesar went out onto the streets in the evening. In a way, it was like working in the fields again. But this time, he was planting seeds for hope and action.

The deadline for voter registration was less than three months away. People who weren't registered couldn't vote in the upcoming elections of 1952. Cesar was out every night leading up to the deadline. He explained to people the benefits of voting. Cesar and the CSO helped to sign up six thousand new voters. In November of 1952, many of these Mexican

Americans voted for the first time. But it wasn't easy. Some election officials challenged the first-time voters. The officials questioned whether the Mexican Americans could read or write. Many of the people were confused and angry. They left without voting.

Cesar had worked hard to get so many people signed up. But the work wasn't over. Ross told Cesar that they could protest the actions of the election officials. They could send a complaint to the attorney general, or leading law enforcer, of California. The attorney general could investigate the officials. Some CSO members had government jobs. They didn't want to sign a written complaint because they were afraid they would get in trouble. But Cesar knew it had to be done, so he signed the protests.

MAKING HEADLINES

The election complaints made headlines in California newspapers. Cesar's name appeared in print for the first time. The accused officials responded by saying the CSO had registered dead people and undocumented immigrants (people who were living in the United States without proper legal papers).

One day, Cesar's boss at the lumberyard told him that agents from the Federal Bureau of Investigation (FBI) wanted to see him. Within minutes, two FBI agents were asking Cesar questions about Communism. Communism is a form of government that scared many people in the United States during the 1950s and 1960s. Some people believed that anyone who challenged the U.S. government must be a Communist. Being called a Communist by government officials was serious.

Cesar wasn't a Communist, and he said so to the FBI. Despite his denials, a local newspaper called Cesar Chavez a Communist. In the weeks and months that followed, others asked Cesar if he was a Communist. But Cesar's friends and coworkers trusted him. They knew him as a man who worked to help people.

Despite this distraction, Cesar kept on helping people get voting rights. Many of Cesar's neighbors could not read or write English well. Cesar showed them how to apply for U.S. citizenship. He helped them understand government papers. He also taught them how to avoid people who tried to take advantage of them. Whatever the problem, Cesar offered to help.

THE RED SCARE

During World War II, the United States and the Soviet Union had fought on the same side. But the two countries had very different government systems. The United States has a capitalist system, in which privately owned businesses set prices and run the economy. The Soviet Union, which broke up in 1991, had a Communist system in which the government owned all businesses and set all prices.

Beginning in the late 1940s, the two countries were at odds. Propaganda—information that wasn't necessarily true—against the Soviet Union started to appear in U.S. newspapers. American newspapers often called the Soviets "reds." Red is an important color for Communist countries. It was the main color of the Soviet Union's flag. The country's army was the Red Army. The fear of the spread of Communist ideas was called the "red scare." People who tried to find Communists in America and send them to prison were known as "red baiters." Cesar Chavez was a target of red baiters for many years.

Red was the main color of the Soviet Union's flag.

Cesar _(second from right)_ was one of many CSO organizers.

If he didn't know how to help, he asked Fred Ross. Cesar went back to people and told them what he had learned. The word spread. People in the area knew that if they needed help, they should talk to Cesar Chavez.

More and more people wanted Cesar's help. He gave his time and advice freely. Then, when he needed volunteers to help with CSO meetings, he called upon those he had helped. These meetings, held in the volunteer's house, gave the organization a family atmosphere. People shared their problems and listened to one another. They planned social get-togethers, such as dinners and dances.

With Fred's training and advice, Cesar helped the groups elect their own officers. The process— from house meetings to the election of officers— usually took about three months. Then Cesar would move on to another neighborhood to help start another CSO group.

On His Own

Saul Alinsky, who was one of the bosses at CSO, liked what Chavez was doing around San Jose. When the lumberyard started laying off employees, Cesar found himself out of a job. That didn't last long. Alinsky and Ross knew Chavez was ready to handle full-time work with the CSO in San Jose. With a growing family, Cesar couldn't refuse the job offer. Soon he faced even more responsibility.

Cesar Chavez had shown he could get people organized in small towns and neighborhoods in and around San Jose. Ross and Alinsky wondered if he could do the same thing by himself in a big city.

ROSS AND ALINSKY

Fred Ross was born in San Francisco in 1910 but grew up in Los Angeles. In 1937, he graduated from the University of Southern California with degrees in English literature and social science. He wanted to be a teacher, but the Great Depression made it hard to find a job. Instead, he worked for the state of California and for the U.S. government. He had jobs that eased relations between tense communities and that helped neighborhoods to fight unfair practices.

After World War II, he met Saul Alinsky. The two set up the first CSOs. Ross went on to train many other CSO members, including Cesar Chavez, in organizing local CSO groups. In the 1960s, he worked with Cesar in setting up strikes. He later ran political campaigns and taught courses in the techniques of organizing communities for political action.

Saul Alinsky was born in 1909. By the early 1920s, he was researching the causes of urban unrest in Chicago, Illinois. Through his study, he realized that poverty left people open to negative ways to get money. He decided that the only solution was for low-income neighborhoods in big cities to become politically powerful. The right to vote was the main political tool these neighborhoods had.

Saul Alinsky

When Alinsky hooked up with Ross, both men had long been working to help those without power get power. Their work in organizing communities—little by little, and with strong training techniques—became one model for urban reform.

They decided to send him to Oakland,
California. This large city is north of San Jose.
They would quickly find out whether Cesar could
be as effective an organizer there. His salary was
thirty-five dollars a week. It was more money than
he had ever earned.

Cesar wondered if he
was ready. He talked to
Helen about the job. As
usual, she stood behind
him. So did his parents
and his brothers and
sisters. Their support
helped Cesar decide. He
accepted the position.

IT'S A FACT!

Throughout his life,
Cesar Chavez never
made more than six
thousand dollars per
year, usually much
less. Helen worked in
the fields to add to
the family's income.

Father Gerald Cox, a
local priest, helped Chavez set up the first house
meeting in Oakland. On the night of the meeting,
Cesar had to force himself to go inside. Most of the
people there were middle-aged women. Twenty-five-
year-old Cesar, five feet six inches tall and skinny,
stood in a dark corner. He watched and listened.

Finally, Cesar spoke. The people looked at
him. They wondered who this young man was and
what he could really know. Cesar explained how

the CSO worked and what it could do to help them. He searched for the right words but worried that no one was paying attention. In his mind, the meeting was a disaster. Yet before the people left, they were talking about having more meetings. Whether they felt sorry for Cesar or honestly felt the evening was useful, they still wanted to meet again. Another seed was planted.

5

MAKING PROGRESS

IN THE WEEKS THAT FOLLOWED, Cesar organized one meeting after another. Each night, after everyone was gone, he thought about what was said. He tried to figure out what made people become silent and what made them argue. Cesar wondered if he could have been a better leader. He was rarely happy with his performance.

After three months of individual house meetings in Oakland, Cesar planned a big group gathering at a hall belonging to Saint Mary's Church. This church was in a low-income part of Oakland and worked with local leaders to improve living conditions.

When Cesar Chavez took over local organizing efforts, he relied on the help of many volunteers.

Cesar told everyone to spread the word. A good turnout would mean people had real interest in gaining some political power for Mexican Americans in the area. Nervously, Cesar hoped people would come.

Only twenty people had arrived at the hall by the time the meeting was scheduled to begin.

Cesar thought it was going to be a disaster. But as the night went on, more people came. Soon more than three hundred people filled the hall. Cesar's fears disappeared, and he smiled as he looked at the crowd.

Fred Ross smiled too when he heard the news. Until that night, Fred had always set up and planned the big meetings. Cesar had shown he could do that on his own. It was a big step.

New Goals

An even bigger step followed. Ross was happy with the reports of the meeting at Saint Mary's. He wanted to give Cesar a new goal. He sent him to Madera and the surrounding San Joaquin Valley. This area in central California has some of the state's best farmland. The territory was bigger and so was the pay. From thirty-five dollars a week, Cesar's salary jumped to fifty-eight dollars. Cesar hadn't even asked for the raise. He thought he was overpaid already. But Saul Alinsky disagreed and insisted that Cesar accept the extra money.

The raise in pay was a huge help. Cesar and Helen now had four children. Fernando, Sylvia,

Linda, and Eloise all joined their parents in moving to Madera. Cesar wished he had more time to spend with his family, but his job often kept him away from home.

From Madera, Cesar took his family farther south, to Hanford and Bakersfield. At each stop, the forceful and energetic organizer planted seeds for the CSO. He started house meetings, set up citizenship classes, and put on voter-registration drives. Within a few months, he would move on to another town. When it was a choice of moving his family or traveling alone, Cesar went alone. He missed his family, yet he hated to have them always packing and leaving a place. That was too much like being a migrant family. Cesar Chavez had put that part of his life behind him. He wanted to do all he could to help those who had to live that way.

THE OXNARD PROBLEM

In 1958, Cesar went to Oxnard, California, a town about thirty-five miles north of Los Angeles. As a boy, Cesar had spent a foggy, wet winter in Oxnard, under terrible working conditions. Cesar was back to help register voters.

Braceros farm by hand in the fields of California.

Cesar discovered a big problem when he got to Oxnard. Local growers didn't hire Mexican Americans who lived in the area. Instead, the owners brought in braceros, migrant workers from Mexico. Braceros would work longer hours at lower wages. Federal laws said that growers could use braceros only if no local workers were available. The growers were breaking the law.

To be sure of the situation, Cesar applied as a worker himself. First, he went to a labor camp where he knew braceros worked. He was told to go back into town to the office of the Farm Placement Service, or FPS. By the time he got to the office and filled out the forms, hours had passed. When he was finally ready to work, Cesar found that braceros had taken all the jobs. Braceros didn't have to go to the FPS office to fill out forms.

IT'S A FACT!

The word *bracero* comes from the Spanish verb *bracear*, which means to swing one's arms. It can also mean to swim using the crawl stroke.

Cesar and the other residents were told to try again the next day. But Cesar had seen enough. He quickly set up a rally of Mexican Americans living in and around Oxnard.

On January 15, 1959, about 1,500 people gathered to hear Cesar speak. His volunteers passed out leaflets that protested the actions of the farm owners. Cesar called the governor's office and California's Department of Employment. He told other Mexican Americans in the area to apply for work as he did. When they were refused jobs too, he had more proof of unfair hiring.

Cesar and other CSO officials convinced FPS
leaders to hire three local workers to harvest crops.
Soon the three were let go. One was fired for lack
of experience, even though he had worked in the
fields for seventeen years.

LEADING THE PROTEST

Cesar continued to fight. He led Mexican
Americans in picketing, or marching in front of,
the FPS office. He also picketed the labor camps
where braceros stayed overnight. The protesters
carried signs that said, "We want jobs!" and "We
deserve to work!"

Cesar called every newspaper reporter and
TV person in the area. He asked them to be at
the FPS office in Oxnard the next morning. They
were there when Cesar and about seventy of his
volunteers filled out work applications. No one
expected to be hired, and no one was.

From the FPS office, Cesar led his group—and
the reporters—to a nearby ranch. A man named
Jones owned the sprawling ranch and hired
braceros every day.

When Cesar's marchers approached the Jones
ranch, many asked what they should do next.

Farmworkers gather to protest low wages.

At the gate, one angry man leaped on top of a car. He urged the marchers to go onto the ranch. Cesar jumped on top of another car. He wanted no part of a violent demonstration.

The people stood behind Cesar. Sensing the people's support, Cesar said that they should never have to register to work again. With reporters recording every moment, Cesar told the workers to burn their registration forms. Once everything had burned, Cesar decided that they had done enough that day.

In the weeks that followed, nothing seemed to happen. Then Cesar learned that James Mitchell, the U.S. secretary of labor, was going to speak in nearby Ventura, California. Cesar quickly organized a march. One thousand Mexican Americans greeted Mitchell when his plane landed at the airport. They followed Mitchell into town. By nightfall, the candle-carrying marchers moved into Oxnard, singing Mexican hymns. When the police threatened to arrest Cesar for leading an illegal parade, he would not step aside. If the police arrested Cesar Chavez, his followers insisted that they be arrested too.

The police couldn't do much. Their jail would never hold all the protesters. Cesar and his followers marched forward with a police escort to protect them.

Slowly, area growers gave in. They even agreed to hire people right out of the CSO office. The FPS made changes too. The agency removed some top officers from their jobs.

IT'S A FACT!

CSO thought its main mission was to help people in cities. Cesar felt his own mission was to help people who worked in the fields.

Encouraged by his successes at Oxnard, Cesar asked the CSO to start a union for farmworkers. The people who worked the soil needed better working conditions. They should have fair pay and benefits, such as insurance to pay them if they got hurt and couldn't work anymore. But Cesar's calls for a union were ignored. Saul Alinsky and other CSO officials said that the CSO could provide farmworkers with the tools to help themselves. To Alinsky and others, a union was unnecessary.

Cesar had learned a great deal in Oxnard. For the first time, he had felt capable of organizing and

"THE HARVEST OF SHAME"

In 1960, a TV special called "The Harvest of Shame" was aired across America. Edward R. Murrow, a famous radio and TV journalist, hosted the program. The show introduced Americans to the hardships that migrant farmworkers faced in Florida and California. It revealed the terrible housing, the lack of education for migrant children, and the hopelessness of migrant families. After the special, reporters came to Delano to talk with Cesar.

leading. He had organized marches and had gotten media publicity. He had known just how far to go to reach his goals. Cesar remained convinced that a union of farmworkers could achieve its own goals by doing the same things. He just needed to convince others of the need.

"VIVA LA CAUSA!"

THE LEADERS OF THE CSO KNEW Cesar was unhappy with their view of a union. But they didn't want to lose his talents. To make sure he stayed with the CSO, they offered him a position as national director in Los Angeles. They also increased his pay to $150 a week.

Cesar accepted the offer. His family had expanded to eight children—Fernando, Sylvia, Linda, Eloise, Elizabeth, Paul, Anna, and Anthony. Helen had sacrificed a great deal so that Cesar could travel and work with his people. She was at home to care for the children, whenever they had problems or needs. Cesar wanted to offer his wife and family all that he could.

Cesar and Helen relax with two of their eight children and a young friend in the 1960s.

Cesar continued to work for the CSO. But some of his energy and excitement left him. He visited Oxnard six months after he'd helped win more rights for workers. He found that everything had returned to the way it was before his effort. The braceros were back working in the fields. The farm owners did as they pleased.

LEAVING THE CSO

By 1962, Cesar had become convinced that no lasting changes would happen for the farmworkers unless they were organized into a union. After many sleepless nights, he made a big decision. With Helen's support and more than one thousand dollars in the bank, Cesar quit his job with the CSO. He was going to try to form a farmworkers' union. It was a huge risk, and Cesar was very frightened about the change.

IT'S A FACT!

For a farmworker, one thousand dollars was a lot of money in 1962. This is about six thousand dollars in the 2000s.

Cesar packed up his family and returned to Delano, near Helen's family. If times got too bad, Helen's family could help. Cesar laid out a map of all eighty-six towns and farmworkers' camps in the area. He promised to visit every one of them. His goal was to encourage workers to form a new union. It would be called the National Farm Workers Association, or NFWA.

Others had tried to organize farmworkers in the past, but they had never really succeeded. The Agricultural Workers Organizing Committee (AWOC) had formed in 1959. Its members were mostly Filipino Americans, and few Mexican Americans had joined that union. It was also part of the AFL-CIO, a huge national labor federation. Cesar believed that joining a big federation was a bad idea. He wanted his people to run their own organization and reach their own goals. At the age of thirty-five, Cesar wanted to form an independent union.

Cesar set up his office in his garage. He copied information about the NFWA on an old copy machine. He took his materials on the road. Wherever he could find an interested farm laborer or two, he stopped to talk about the new union.

Cesar's energy and interest won him valuable assistants. Dolores Huerta, one of the CSO's top workers, joined Chavez. So did Wayne C. Hartmire,

Cesar *(far left)* turned to the Reverend Wayne C. Hartmire *(right)* and others for help with building the farmworkers' union.

a Protestant minister. Cesar had been most effective
at attracting Catholic migrants. Hartmire was good at
bringing in other types of Christian migrants. Cesar's

DOLORES HUERTA

Born in 1930 in New Mexico, Dolores Huerta was a big part of the
early success of the NFWA (National Farm Workers Association). She
first met Cesar Chavez in the late 1950s, when both were working for
CSO (Community Service Organization). She became a CSO lobbyist (a
person who persuades lawmakers to vote for certain laws) in
Sacramento, California. She worked to ease some of the problems that
kept farmworkers from voting.

In 1962, Cesar and Dolores both left CSO and set up the NFWA [later called

the UFW (United Farm Workers)].
Dolores organized the group's strikes.
She represented the farmworkers
when they were setting up contracts
with grape growers. With Cesar, she
created the first medical and pension
plans for farmworkers. She came out
against the use of pesticides,
chemicals that hurt the health of
farmworkers. For more than forty
years, she has worked hard to gain
rights for farmworkers and to
establish equality for women.

**Dolores Huerta worked with
Cesar Chavez to form a union
for farmworkers.**

cousin Manuel gave up a steady job selling cars
in San Diego to help.

Not everyone was so easily convinced.
Earlier efforts to gain
rights for farmworkers
had failed. Government
officials and growers had
been able to block
anyone trying to bring
the migrants together as
an organized group. Even
the National Labor
Relations Act, which
protected most laborers,

IT'S A FACT!

The National Labor
Relations Act was
passed in 1935. It
protected the rights
of labor unions to
organize and to work
together to get
better wages.

didn't help farmworkers. Some people wondered
how Chavez could make a difference.

But Cesar was serious, and he never
promised quick solutions. He simply kept
organizing people. When people learned he had
given up a good job to organize farmworkers,
they were even more impressed.

GOALS AND DREAMS

On September 30, 1962, Cesar Chavez took
another big step. He called together all interested

farmworkers for a meeting in an old theater in
Fresno, California. Fresno is a city at the center of
California's farmland. More than two hundred
people attended this first official convention of the
NFWA. Cesar led the meeting, sharing his goals
and dreams. Working together, Cesar said,
farmworkers could meet those goals.

Dolores Huerta spoke too, backing up Cesar's
ideas and plans. Manuel Chavez had another
surprise—a flag for the union. The deep red flag had
a black eagle on a white circle. Cesar considered
the eagle to be a symbol of strength and hope.

Cesar didn't want people viewing his union
as just another labor group. He wanted the
NFWA to be a community. Like most unions, it
would have a constitution and officers. Members
would have to pay money, or dues, to join. But
the NFWA would be an organization that fought
for the needs of its members. As the early
members elected leaders, they built the
framework for their group. *Viva la causa!* or "Long
live the cause!" was chosen as the group's motto.
The group decided that dues would be three dollars
and fifty cents per month. For low-paid migrant
workers of the time, this was a lot of money.

THE FARMWORKERS' FLAG

Some people disliked the flag Cesar had chosen for the NFWA. They thought it looked like the symbol of Nazi Germany, against whom the United States had fought in World War II. But Manuel Chavez explained that the colors stood for important things. The black eagle represented the farmworkers'

dark and grim situation. The white circle stood for hope. The red background reminded union members of the hard sacrifices they would have to make to be successful.

But they believed that the money would be well spent. They were investing in their future.

The convention in Fresno was a great success. Yet within months, many of those who had signed up at the beginning left the group. The number of paying members dropped from two hundred to twelve. Cesar wondered if the union would survive. Many people came, asked questions, got answers, and then dropped out. At times, Cesar felt alone in trying to hold the union together. He promised to give the cause three full years. If the NFWA wasn't a united group by then, he would give up.

Cesar worked even harder. He drove around California to meet with farmworkers. He listened for hours to their concerns. He made sure he completely understood what was important to them. He reminded them that working together could bring results. The work was tiring, but slowly and steadily the NFWA membership grew. Cesar looked for a chance to attract even more attention. That chance came in September 1965.

7 THE DELANO GRAPE STRIKE

AMONG THE WORST spots for migrants to work were the vineyards around Delano. In hot temperatures, grape pickers hunched over for hours, picking fruit. The pay wasn't good. Vineyard workers sometimes found themselves covered with insect-killing chemical sprays. Toilets were far away and hard to find. If clean drinking

(Above) **Cesar poses beside a sign that reads** *huelga,* **the Spanish word for strike.**

water was provided, workers often had to rent a cup to drink it.

Despite the bad conditions, workers in the vineyards were luckier than most migrants. Grape cultivation stretched over ten months. This allowed workers time to stay in one place. But in September of 1965, the growers cut already low wages. The workers were ready to rebel. The members of the mostly Filipino AWOC called a strike for September 8.

IT'S A FACT!

Wages for farmworkers are low. In 1965, the average yearly income of California farm laborers was $1,350 (about $7,500 in the 2000s). This figure was well below the poverty line of $3,100 ($17,000) set by the government.

JOINING THE STRIKE

Larry Itliong, the AWOC's leader, went to Cesar Chavez. He believed that Cesar would want to help the AWOC get better wages and treatment for the grape pickers. Itliong asked Cesar if the NFWA would join the AWOC in the strike.

Cesar left the decision up to the NFWA members. He presented the reasons for the strike at a meeting on September 16, Mexican Independence Day. Everyone agreed. The NFWA would help the AWOC workers in their fight against the growers.

Few thought that the grape pickers' strike would finish quickly. The vineyard owners were rich and could hold out for a long time. Although the workers were poor, they were willing to do whatever it took—and for as long as it took—to get the changes they wanted.

Cesar knew it was important to involve more than just the NFWA, the AWOC, and the growers in this strike. If people understood the problems of the vineyard workers, they might pressure the growers to bargain with the workers.

In the following weeks, Cesar took his cause to anyone who would listen. He not only talked about the strike against the vineyard owners, he also talked about the needs of all farmworkers. He spoke of a worker's right to be respected and about the low wages paid to farmworkers.

While Cesar worked to make people more aware of the farmworkers' struggles, he also thought of other ways to show their needs. After studying the situation, Cesar decided that focusing on one grower would be wiser than going after all of them.

Together, the growers were rich and powerful, but if one gave in, others might follow. With other strike leaders, Cesar selected Schenley Industries, Inc., in Delano as a target. Picketers showed up outside Schenley's large farm. The NFWA and the AWOC urged everyone to boycott, or refuse to buy, Schenley products.

MARCHING FOR RIGHTS

From his readings, Chavez remembered that nonviolent marches had worked well for Mohandas Gandhi in India. He also knew that black civil rights leaders in the southern United States, such as Dr. Martin Luther King Jr., were

Dr. Martin Luther King Jr. *(center)* leads a march in the 1960s supporting the rights of African Americans.

leading their supporters on marches. These leaders were demanding that blacks receive equal opportunities. He wondered if such marches could help the farmworkers of California. After careful thought, he decided that it was worth a try.

Cesar Chavez makes a speech during a grape boycott in 1965.

He called upon NFWA members to stage peaceful marches on agricultural offices around the state. In March of 1966, he started a march

Cesar *(far right)* marches with NFWA members to Sacramento. The march drew public attention to the problems of the striking grape pickers.

from Delano to the California state Capitol in Sacramento, a distance of about three hundred miles. The purpose was to ask Governor Edmund G. "Pat" Brown to hear union demands and to help settle the strike.

Sixty-seven people began the march, gathering other people as they went. The marchers carried U.S., Mexican, and NFWA flags. Some also carried banners with the image of the Virgin of Guadalupe. By the time the farmworkers reached Sacramento on Easter Sunday, a crowd of ten thousand was waiting. They cheered the travelers, causing the exhausted Cesar Chavez to flash a wide smile.

IT'S A FACT!

The long march was hard on Cesar's body. His ankle and then his leg swelled up. Sometimes he had to be driven behind the rest of the marchers. Other times he used a cane for support.

The march was a success. It had gained publicity for the strikers and had attracted the attention of government officials in California and in Washington, D.C. The pressure was on the vineyard owners. After talks with the leaders of Schenley

Industries, Cesar announced that the company had
agreed to recognize the NFWA as a union.

Under the new contract, farmworkers at
Schenley earned a pay raise of thirty-five cents an
hour. The company also promised to give
regularly to the NFWA credit union, a bank set up
just for NFWA members. It was the first union
contract for farmworkers in U.S. history. Chavez's
cheerful face appeared in newspapers and
magazines around the country.

FIGHTING DIGIORGIO

Grateful for the publicity, Cesar knew there was
much more to do. Schenley Industries was just the
first step. A week after the Delano march ended,
Cesar mapped out plans to go after another major
farm near Delano, the Sierra Vista acreage run by
the DiGiorgio Corporation. He asked people to
boycott DiGiorgio products and told his NFWA
followers to picket outside Sierra Vista.

DiGiorgio got a court order that said only a
few picketers could gather at a time. To get
around the order, NFWA supporters began
praying at a makeshift chapel Richard Chavez had
created in the back of his station wagon. The

chapel honored the Virgin of Guadalupe. NFWA members came in large groups to pray or listen to Mass. They recruited new members from among the farmworkers.

While Chavez talked to DiGiorgio officials, another union took action. Cesar had shown that farmworkers could be organized and powerful. The Teamsters, a union that represented people who worked in transport, wanted to grab the farmworkers' dues and power. Teamsters' leaders hoped to pull NFWA and AWOC members away from their unions. DiGiorgio let the Teamsters talk to its farmworkers, but the company wouldn't let in the NFWA and the AWOC.

Cesar objected to this unfair treatment. Governor Brown set up a committee to review the situation. It granted the NFWA and the AWOC the right to talk to the DiGiorgio workers. The committee also said a secret ballot would decide which union would represent the farmworkers.

At the same time, the AFL-CIO suggested that the NFWA should join with the AWOC. Chavez agreed, and the United Farm Workers Organizing Committee (UFWOC) was born. In August 1966, when farmworkers at DiGiorgio's were allowed to

choose between the Teamsters and the newly
formed union, the UFWOC was the easy choice.

Cesar's work brought him the attention of
lawmakers in the U.S. Congress. Senator Robert
F. Kennedy came to Delano to talk with Cesar.
They discussed the needs of the farmworkers and
the purpose of strikes, pickets, and boycotts.

THE AFL-CIO VS. THE TEAMSTERS

The AFL-CIO is a federation, or grouping, of unions. Many different
unions, including the Teamsters, belong to the AFL-CIO. In the 1950s, the
Teamsters was the country's largest union. It represented people who
drove trucks and cars, who built automobiles, who processed food, and
who brewed beer.

In 1957, the AFL-CIO and the U.S. government accused Teamsters'
leaders of illegal practices. The federation expelled the Teamsters, which
operated on its own until 1987. While Cesar was building the NFWA, the
Teamsters and the AFL-CIO were competing against one another for
union contracts. The more union contracts each group got, the more
powerful they became. Cesar felt the Teamsters represented the growers,
not the migrant workers. He believed that the Teamsters used threats to
make farmworkers join the union.

Cesar wanted the NFWA to stay independent. But he also wanted the
union to win out over the Teamsters. Combining forces would benefit
both the NFWA and the AWOC. Together, their bigger union could
challenge the Teamsters. Cesar and Larry Itliong combined their unions
in 1966 to form the United Farm Workers Organizing Committee
(UFWOC).

Senator Robert F. Kennedy supported Cesar Chavez and his efforts to help farmworkers.

Kennedy pledged Cesar his support. Dr. King also gave Cesar encouragement to continue working for equal rights.

BOYCOTTING AND FASTING

In 1967, the UFWOC targeted yet another large California grape grower, Giumarra. Cesar called for a boycott of Giumarra's grapes. But the company fought back. It put labels from many different grape growers on its boxes of grapes. People buying grapes couldn't tell who had grown them. After much discussion, the NFWOC decided to extend the boycott. The union asked people throughout the United States to stop buying all grapes grown in California. Soon pro-NFWOC picketers were showing up at supermarkets in large U.S. cities. The boycott spread quickly.

Although Cesar was happy with the union's progress, changes came slowly. Some UFWOC supporters suggested that violence might result in faster action. Cesar quickly put that idea aside. Instead, he once again followed the example of Mohandas Gandhi, who often fasted (stopped eating) as a form of protest. On February 15, 1968, Cesar Chavez began a fast. This dramatic action captured headlines around the country. As Cesar's fasting continued, more and more people followed his weakening condition. Many people wondered what was driving him to this action.

More donations flowed in to help the UFWOC. Pressure increased for the growers to give in. In Europe, dockworkers refused to unload California grapes from ships. Twenty-five days later, Cesar was satisfied that he had shown people the value of nonviolent action. He finally started eating again. To mark the end of the fast, Robert Kennedy offered Cesar a small bit of bread. Then the two leaders, along with thousands of supporters, celebrated Mass.

By the spring of 1969, after four years of picketing, marching, and fasting, Cesar was tired. Yet he stood firm. Cesar asked people across the nation to buy only grapes boxed with the UFWOC black eagle emblem. Any other grapes should be

Cesar showed the strain of his fast in 1968.

In 1970, several of California's biggest grape growers, represented by John Giumarra (right), signed a contract with the United Farm Workers Organizing Committee.

boycotted. Because of the efforts of Cesar Chavez and his followers, many people backed the boycott. Vineyard owners complained that the boycotting was costing them twenty-five million dollars. One by one, the growers agreed to the UFWOC's demands. In July of 1970, five years after the strike had begun, it ended. Most grape growers agreed to three-year contracts offering better wages, health insurance, and benefits.

This major victory was soon followed by a strike by lettuce workers in the Salinas Valley of California. Cesar knew the new strike would be a challenge, but he felt sure of himself. That confidence rose every time he saw the flying black eagle on a box of grapes. To Cesar Chavez, the UFWOC emblem didn't just stand for the men and women who had picked those grapes. It also reflected new rights and respect for all farmworkers, as well as better pay.

8 CONTINUING THE STRUGGLE

IN THE SUMMER OF 1970, fourteen large lettuce growers in the Salinas Valley signed contracts with the Teamsters. The deals were good for the transportation union and the growers. But farmworkers had not been allowed to vote because they were not members of the Teamsters union. They gained little under the new contracts.

Cesar Chavez arrived on the scene to organize UFWOC members to fight both the Teamsters and the growers. On August 8, 1970, Chavez called a strike against the Salinas division of the Purex Company. His plan to single out one grower had worked in Delano, so he thought it was worth trying again. Within two weeks, the lettuce grower shut down. But the Teamsters and the other growers stood firm.

Soon Cesar took another step. He called for a general strike of all lettuce workers in the Salinas Valley. About seven thousand workers stayed home, and forty farms were left without pickers. With the public starting to take an interest, Cesar asked people to boycott the lettuce of Bud Antle, another grower who had signed up with the Teamsters. Antle fought back, going to court to stop Chavez's boycott. Cesar refused to change his mind, even when he was threatened with jail.

RAISING THE STAKES

On December 4, 1970, he stood in a Salinas courtroom. More than two thousand supporters crowded into the area. The people overflowed onto the surrounding block. As always, according to Cesar's orders, they were silent and nonviolent. Even when he was sent to jail, the farmworkers stood quietly.

In the meantime, UFWOC lawyers took Cesar's case to the California Supreme Court. The higher court ordered that Chavez be released on

IT'S A FACT!

Cesar set up a strict schedule while in jail. He planned his reading, eating, and sleeping periods. He made time for exercise, writing, and meditation. Visits were scheduled. His supporters set up picket lines around the jail. They sang hymns and shouted cheers.

Christmas Eve while judges reviewed the case. Four months later, the court ruled that the UFWOC boycott against lettuce growers was legal. Cesar Chavez was cleared of any charges.

At about that time, the Teamsters seemed to self-destruct. Union leaders were found guilty of misusing funds and carrying weapons. The Teamsters were suddenly more worried about their own organization. Their fight with the UFWOC was over.

But the lettuce growers held out. Cesar decided to call a nationwide boycott of lettuce. He planned to continue the boycott until the growers recognized the union. He felt like he was making progress, but everything always seemed to take so long. But Cesar was willing to put in whatever time it took. Working eighteen hours a day, he bounced around the country, going wherever he was asked or needed.

The union's lettuce boycott spread to the subways of New York City.

DANGERS AND HEADLINES

Cesar believed in his cause, but some people
questioned his devotion. Some people said that he
wanted to run the UFWOC by himself without
sharing power. Some people
felt Cesar was too
demanding. Others said he
was arrogant.

Some people wanted
Cesar out of the way no
matter what it took. Death
threats came in the mail
and on the telephone.
Cesar couldn't be sure who was sending the threats.
It could be angry growers or Teamsters. Cesar's
friends worried about his safety. Cesar also worried
about his enemies.

It's a Fact!

Cesar eventually got
two German
shepherd watchdogs.
He named them
Boycott and Huelga.

Despite the dangers, Cesar continued to
strengthen the farmworkers' union. In 1972, the
UFWOC became an independent partner within
the powerful AFL-CIO and was officially renamed
the United Farm Workers. This partnership gave
the UFW more political power.

Slowly, Cesar's efforts won the support of
politicians. He fought for laws that would ensure

Cesar poses with Boycott and Huelga.

workers had safe and clean working conditions. In the summer of 1975, the UFW scored a major victory when California Governor Edmund G. "Jerry" Brown signed the Agricultural Labor Relations Act. It said that a union of farmworkers had the right to bargain with growers.

On March 10, 1977, Cesar got more headlines. After almost ten years of argument, he helped patch up differences separating the UFW and the Teamsters. Farmworkers felt free to join the UFW, if they wanted. Membership in the UFW grew quickly.

Throughout the 1970s, Cesar *(right)* continued to lead boycotts and pickets to protest unfair labor conditions.

IT'S A FACT!

In 1975, with the political support of the UFW, use of the short-handled hoe was outlawed. Using this tool puts very hard pressure on the backs of the farmworkers.

Free from having to compete with the Teamsters, Cesar could focus on helping farmworkers and stopping abuses.

In 1980, Cesar's farmworkers' union celebrated its fifteenth birthday. During those years, hourly pay for members had climbed from less than a dollar to five dollars an hour. Farmworkers got covered by medical insurance and had unemployment benefits. They were part of retirement programs. They also had ways to challenge abuses by employers.

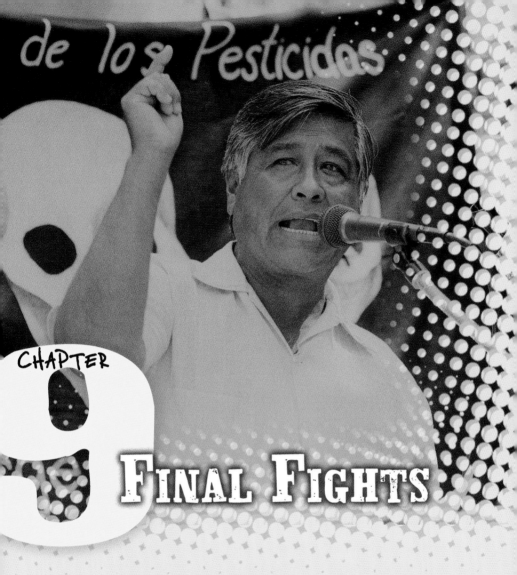

CHAPTER 9

FINAL FIGHTS

(Above) During the 1980s, Cesar spoke out about the dangers of pesticide use.

CESAR WAS WORRIED about the health and safety of farmworkers. He took an interest in pesticides. These are chemicals growers use to fight insects. One study of pesticide use in the mid-1980s was especially troubling. Farmworkers in the San Joaquin Valley of

California showed higher-than-average cancer rates. Scientific studies pointed to pesticides as the likely cause. Cesar asked people to stop buying grapes grown on farms that used pesticides.

STILL SPREADING THE WORD

Again, Cesar turned to fasting as a means to focus attention on the boycott. His doctors disapproved, but he would not give in. On July 17, 1988, Cesar stopped eating.

Although there was some media interest in Cesar's fasting, people did not seem as concerned as they once had been. Times had changed. The public had seen world leaders— such as Martin Luther King Jr. and Robert Kennedy—assassinated. Wars had cost thousands of American lives. Television and newspapers published stories every day of violent crimes. The

IT'S A FACT!

After Cesar finished his fast, other people fasted in support of the pesticide cause. Well-known people around the country— including Jesse Jackson, Whoopi Goldberg, and Carly Simon—went on mini-fasts that lasted three days. Each person passed the fast on to the next person.

report of one man fasting on behalf of farmworkers did not seem as important as it had years before.

On August 21, 1988, Anthony and Paul Chavez, Cesar's sons, helped their weakened father to a chair on a stage in Delano. Cesar's doctors had finally convinced him that he might

After his fast in 1988, a weakened Cesar Chavez received support from the Reverend Jesse Jackson.

soon die if he didn't end his thirty-six-day fast. Helen stood by with Ethel Kennedy, Robert's widow, and Cesar's ninety-six-year-old mother, Juana. The Reverend Jesse Jackson, a civil rights leader, promised to carry on the farmworkers' fight.

TOWARD THE SUNSET

Cesar Chavez never fully regained his strength after the fast. He continued his work on behalf of the UFW, but he was less active. His steps were slow, and his voice was less full. Meetings, speeches, and award ceremonies continued, but Cesar tired quickly.

As Cesar grew weaker, the UFW membership decreased. At one time, more than seventy thousand people had been members. By the early 1990s, that number had slipped to less than ten thousand. Cesar was unhappy with the situation, but he seemed helpless to do anything about it.

IT'S A FACT!

In 1991, the Mexican government awarded Cesar the Aguila Azteca, which means Aztec Eagle. This award goes to people of Mexican heritage who have achieved great things outside of Mexico.

In the spring of 1993, Cesar Chavez returned to the place of his birth near Yuma, Arizona. A large grower who owned property in Arizona and California was suing UFW workers. Cesar was called in to speak in court for the farmworkers.

Visiting the Yuma area brought back many memories. The loss of his family's farm during the Great Depression more than fifty years before had changed his life. But it was not Cesar's nature to dwell upon the past. Instead, he laid out plans to help farmworkers in the area.

Despite the danger to his health, Cesar decided to fast again, hoping to draw attention to the trial.

Cesar continued to lead protests in the 1990s.

Each day, newspapers and TV stations reported on his health condition and the courtroom action. Many reporters traced Cesar's life, from his beginning above his parents' store to his national fame as a leader for farmworkers. Some repeated claims that he was demanding and stubborn.

Staying at a friend's home, Cesar went to bed early on the night of April 22, 1993. The next morning, he was found dead in his room. He was sixty-six years old.

Honoring Cesar

During his life, Cesar Chavez had led many marches, but none was as long as the one that took place after his death. In buses and beat-up trucks, by car and on foot, the people came to say good-bye. The crowd numbered about twenty-five thousand.

In ninety-degree heat, the crowd followed Cesar Chavez's coffin from Delano to the UFW buildings, a four-mile march. The mourners carried gladiolas, Helen Chavez's favorite flower. They lifted red and white banners with the black eagle of the UFW.

On a dusty field near the union hall, the people gathered under tents. Many mourners

were well known, including Ethel Kennedy, Jesse
Jackson, former governor Jerry Brown, and actors
Martin Sheen and Edward James Olmos. Most of
the people were just farmworkers. These men and
women had stood beside Cesar Chavez fighting
for workers' rights. After the funeral, they would
return to lives that had been helped by the man
they had come to honor. Cesar Chavez had led
the way.

Soon after Cesar's death, his supporters set up
the Cesar E. Chavez Foundation. Its mission is to

**Twenty-five thousand people marched in Cesar Chavez's
funeral procession.**

show communities how to pull together to reach
their goals of justice and equality. In 1994, U.S.
president Bill Clinton awarded Cesar the
Presidential Medal of
Freedom. Helen Chavez
accepted the award.
California established
Cesar Chavez Day to be
celebrated across the state
on March 31, Cesar's
birthday. Other states have
also named this day as
Cesar Chavez Day.

IT'S A FACT!

A musical play about
Cesar's life, called
Let the Eagle Fly,
was performed in
Chicago, Illinois, in
July 2004.

Communities have named libraries, schools,
and parks after Cesar. In 2003, the U.S. Postal
Service created a stamp in Cesar's honor. But this
great leader once said that the best way to
remember him was to organize. Many people are
making sure his work continues.

1880s Cesario Chavez, Cesar's grandfather, leaves Mexico and begins to farm near Yuma, Arizona.

1927 Cesar Estrada Chavez is born to Librado and Juana Chavez on March 31 near Yuma.

1929 The Great Depression begins.

1937 Librado Chavez loses the family farm.

1938 The Chavez family becomes migrant farmworkers, moving between Arizona and California.

1939 The Chavez family moves to the barrio of Sal Si Puedes in San Jose, California.

1941 The United States enters World War II.

1942 Librado Chavez is badly hurt in a car accident. Cesar decides to leave school to help support the family.

1944 Cesar joins the U.S. Navy. By this time, the family has settled in Delano, California.

1945 World War II ends.

1946 Cesar is discharged from the navy and returns to Delano.

1947 Cesar joins the National Agricultural Workers Union.

1948 Cesar marries Helen Fabela and moves to San Jose.

1952 Cesar meets Father Donald McDonnell. The priest tells Fred Ross, leader of the Community Service Organization (CSO), about Cesar.

1950s Cesar sets up CSO groups throughout California. He meets Dolores Huerta.

1958 Cesar leads the fight against the hiring of braceros in Oxnard, California.

1960s Cesar becomes national director of CSO. Dolores is his assistant. CBS-TV airs "A Harvest of Shame."

1962 Cesar leaves CSO after it refuses to consider forming a farmworkers' union. He sets up the National Farm Workers Association (NFWA). Dolores Huerta also leaves CSO to become NFWA vice president.

1964 The Civil Rights Act is passed. It bans unfair practices in voting and employment.

1965 The NFWA decides to join a grape strike in Delano already in progress by Filipino farmworkers of the Agricultural Workers Organizing Committee (AWOC). The first boycott starts.

1966 Cesar leads a march from Delano to Sacramento, the state capital, to drum up support for the grape strike. Schenley vineyards makes an agreement with the NFWA, the first-ever contract between a grower and a farmworkers' union. The AWOC and the

NFWA merge to form the National Farm Workers
Organizing Committee (NFWOC).

1968 Cesar begins a fast to encourage nonviolence among
union organizers. He breaks the fast with Senator
Robert F. Kennedy. Kennedy is assassinated in
California.

1969 International Grape Boycott Day takes place on
May 10.

1970 Cesar is jailed for not obeying a court order to stop
boycotting lettuce. Many growers sign contracts with
the NFWOC. The first boycott ends.

1972 California voters defeat Proposition 22, a plan to
outlaw boycotting. The NFWOC becomes the UFW
and is chartered within the AFL-CIO. The UFW
calls for a second boycott to protest the growers'
contracts with the Teamsters Union.

1973 UFW and the Teamsters Union compete for the
union membership of farmworkers.

1975 The California Agricultural Labor Relations Act becomes law. It is the first law overseeing the organization of farm laborers. The short-handled hoe is outlawed.

1978 The Teamsters Union stops competing for unionization. The UFW ends the second boycott.

1984 Cesar calls for a third boycott of grapes to highlight the use of dangerous pesticides.

1986 Cesar starts the "Wrath of Grapes" campaign to further highlight pesticide use.

1988 Cesar starts his thirty-six-day Fast for Life in Delano to call attention to farmworkers poisoned by pesticides.

1991 The Mexican government awards Cesar the Aguila Azteca, the highest award given to a nonmilitary person.

1993 Cesar dies on April 23 near Yuma. Thousands go to his funeral. The Chavez family sets up the Cesar E. Chavez Foundation.

1994 Helen Chavez accepts the Presidential Medal of Freedom for Cesar from President Bill Clinton.

1997 PBS-TV airs *The Fight in the Fields*, a documentary about the farmworkers' movement.

2000 California establishes a state holiday in honor of Cesar. The UFW ends the third boycott after sixteen years.

2003 The U.S. Postal Service issues a stamp in honor of Cesar.

2004 *Let the Eagle Fly*, a musical play based on Cesar's life, is performed in Chicago, Illinois.

AFL-CIO: the initials of the American Federation of Labor and Congress of Industrial Organizations, a grouping of more than sixty unions, created in 1955

barrio: a district or neighborhood, usually with a Spanish-speaking population

boycott: to stop buying or taking part in something as a way of making a protest

bracero: a farmworker from Mexico who is hired to harvest crops

Communist: a person who supports or lives under a government system in which the government owns most property and controls most labor and trade

CSO: the initials of the Community Service Organization, founded by Fred Ross in 1949 to organize Mexican Americans

drought: a long period of very dry weather

fasting: the act of giving up eating for a time

Federal Bureau of Investigation (FBI): the main criminal investigation branch of the U.S. Department of Justice

Great Depression: lasting from about 1929 to 1942, a period of economic hardship in the United States and throughout the world

Hispanic: the culture of countries in Latin American, such as Mexico and Cuba, where Spanish is the major language. The term also names a person whose background is from such countries.

Mexican American: a person born in the United States whose family originally came from Mexico

migrant farmworker: a worker who moves around doing seasonal farmwork, such as harvesting

NFWA: the initials of the National Farm Workers Association, founded by Cesar Chavez in 1962

Presidential Medal of Freedom: the highest nonmilitary award in the United States, given by the president of the United States

racial discrimination: an opinion formed unfairly about a racial group. Racial discrimination can lead to racial segregation, or the practice of keeping racial groups apart.

strike: the act of refusing to work as a way to protest wages or working conditions

Teamsters union: a labor union working for the rights of truck drivers, chauffeurs, and warehouse workers that was first set up in the early 1900s

UFW: the initials of the United Farm Workers, the union formed when the AWOC (Agricultural Workers Organizing Commitee) and the NFWA joined together

union: an organized group of workers that is set up to improve wages and working conditions for the people in the group

voting rights: the legal ability to vote in an election

SELECTED BIBLIOGRAPHY

Adams, John P. "AFL-CIO Organizers Go after Farm Labor." *Business Week*, September 24, 1960.

Allen, Steve. "Migrant Workers in Your State: Must They Work Dirt Cheap?" *Coronet*, March 1967.

Ball, Charles E. "Farm Labor: What You Can Expect from Union Organizers." *Farm Journal*, May 1972.

Black, Roe C. "The Black Eagle Wins." *Time*, August 10, 1970.

Buckley, William F., Jr. "The Chavez Machine." *National Review*, August 10, 1971.

Chavez, Cesar. "Marcher." *New Yorker*, May 17, 1967.

_____. "Nonviolence Still Works." *Look*, April 1, 1969.

Chavez, Cesar, and Bayard Rustin. *Right to Work Laws: A Trap for America's Minorities*. New York: A. Philip Randolph Institute, n.d.

Coles, Robert. *Migrants, Sharecroppers, Mountaineers*. Boston: Little, Brown and Company, 1971.

Day, Mark. *Forty Acres: Cesar Chavez and the Farm Workers*. New York: Praeger, 1971.

Dunne, John Gregory. *Delano: The Story of the California Grape Strike*. Rev. ed. New York: Farrar, Straus & Giroux, 1971.

Dunning, Harold. *Trade Unions and Migrant Workers: A Worker's Educational Guide*. Washington, D.C.: International Labour Office, 1985.

Fodell, Beverly. *Cesar Chavez and the United Farm Workers: A Selective Bibliography*. Detroit: Wayne State University Press, 1974.

Fusco, Paul, and George D. Horowitz. *La Causa: The California Grape Strike*. New York: Collier, 1970.

Gates, David. "A Secular Saint of '60s." *Newsweek,* May 3, 1993.

Goodwin, David. *Cesar Chavez: Hope for the People.* New York: Fawcett, 1991.

Grebler, Leo, Joan W. Moore, and Ralph C. Guzman. *The Mexican-American People: The Nation's Second Largest Minority.* New York: The Gree Press, 1970.

Henninger, Daniel. "And Now, Lettuce." *New Republic,* October 10, 1970.

Levy, Jacques E. *Cesar Chavez: Autobiography of La Causa.* New York: W. W. Norton & Company, Inc., 1975.

Lindsey, Robert. "Cesar Chavez, 66, Organizer of Union for Migrants, Dies." *New York Times,* April 24, 1993.

London, Joan, and Henry Anderson. *So Shall Ye Reap.* New York: Cromwell, 1970.

Matthiessen, Peter. *Sal Si Puedes: Cesar Chavez and the New American Revolution.* Rev. ed. New York: Random House, 1973.

Rodriguez, Consuelo. *Cesar Chavez.* Philadelphia: Chelsea House Publishers, 1991.

Taft, Philip. *Organized Labor in American History.* New York: Harper & Row, 1964.

Taylor, Ronald B. *Chavez and the Farmworkers.* Boston: Beacon Press, 1975.

Terzian, James P., and Kathryn Cramer. *Mighty Hard Road: The Story of Cesar Chavez.* Garden City, NY: Doubleday, 1970.

Yinger, Winthrop. "Viva La Causa." *Christian Century,* August 27, 1969.

Brown, Jonathan A. *Cesar Chavez*. Circle Pines, MN: World Almanac Library, 2004.

The Cesar E. Chavez Foundation
http://www.cesarchavezfoundation.org
The official website of the foundation set up after Chavez's death in 1993 to honor him and his goals. The website features links to ways to celebrate Cesar Chavez Day, resources for further study, and more.

Coleman, Penny. *Strike!* Brookfield, CT: Millbrook Press, 1995.

Fight in the Fields
http://www.pbs.org/itvs/fightfields/resources.html
The website that goes with a PBS program called *Fight in the Fields: Cesar Chavez and the Farmworkers' Struggle.* The website offers suggestions for creative ways to use nonviolence as a form of protest, quotations from Cesar Chavez, and more.

Gaines, Ann. *Cesar E. Chavez: The Fight for Farm Workers' Rights*. Chanhassen, MN: Child's World, 2003.

Gonzales, Doreen. *Cesar Chavez: Leader for Migrant Farm Workers*. Berkeley Heights, NJ: Enslow Publishers, 1996.

Krull, Kathleen. *Harvesting Hope: The Story of Cesar Chavez.* New York: Harcourt, 2003.

Larios, Richard, Rudy Gutierrez, and Dana Catherine De Ruiz. *La Causa: The Migrant Farmworkers' Story*. Austin, TX: Steck-Vaughn, 1992.

Murcia, Rebecca Thatcher. *Dolores Huerta*. Hockessin, DE: Mitchell Lane, 2002.

Paladino, Catherine. *One Good Apple: Growing Our Food for the Sake of the Earth*. Boston: Houghton Mifflin Company, 1999.

Paradigm Productions
http://www.paradigmproductions.org
The website of the company that made the documentary, *Fight in the Fields: Cesar Chavez and the Farmworkers' Struggle*, offers articles by Cesar Chavez, Dolores Huerta, Richard Chavez, and others involved in the struggle for farmworkers' rights.

Sorenson, Margo. *Fight in the Fields: Cesar Chavez*. Des Moines, IA: Perfection Learning, 1998.

Soto, Gary. *Cesar Chavez: A Hero for Everyone*. New York: Aladdin Library, 2003.

———. *Jessie de la Cruz: A Profile of a United Farm Worker*. New York: Persea Books, 2002.

United Farm Workers
http://www.ufw.org
The website of the union set up by Cesar Chavez offers ways to stay informed about issues important to farmworkers, addresses or local offices, and more.

Wheeler, Jill C. *Cesar Chavez*. Edina, MN: Abdo & Daughters, 2003.

PHOTO ACKNOWLEDGMENTS

Photographs are used with the permission of: Library of Congress, p. 4, 10 (LC-DIG-ppmsc-04792), 79 (LC-U9-5415-30); César E. Chávez Foundation, pp. 5, 7, 13, 15, 20, 23, 24, 26, 29, 102; Archives of Labor and Urban Affairs, Walter P. Reuther Library, Wayne State University, pp. 9, 19, 36, 44, 50, 53, 61, 64, 67, 69, 74, 81, 87, 89, 91, 101; National Archives, pp. 12 (NWDNS-83-G-41476), 72 [NWDNS-306-SSM-4C(35)6]; © Bettmann/CORBIS, pp. 21, 46, 63, 82, 92, 94; © CORBIS, p. 30; Illustrated London News Picture Library, p. 33; Getty Images, pp. 39, 73; Hyde Park Press, p. 56; © Mickey Pfleger, p. 90; © Najlah Feanny/CORBIS, p. 96; © 2005 Ilka Hartmann, p. 98. The map on p. 43 is by Laura Westlund.

Cover: © Najlah Feanny/CORBIS.